MONSTER ⚙ MACHINES

RACE CARS

DAVID JEFFERIS

RAINTREE
STECK-VAUGHN
PUBLISHERS

A Harcourt Company

Austin   New York
www.steck-vaughn.com

Library of Congress Cataloging-in-Publication Data

Jefferis, David.
  Racing cars / David Jefferis.
  p. cm.—(Monster machines)
  Includes index.
  ISBN 0-7398-2880-0
  1. Automobiles, Racing—Juvenile literature.
  [1. Automobiles, Racing.
  2. Automobile racing.]
  I. Title. II. Series.

TL236 .J383 2001
629.228—dc21

00-055241

Printed in Singapore
Bound in the United States
1 2 3 4 5 6 7 8 9 0 02 01 00

Acknowledgments
We wish to thank the following individuals and organizations for their help and assistance and for supplying material in their collections: Jorge Alburquerque, All-Sport Photographic Ltd., Tim Andrew, Alpha Archive, Simon Bruty, Jeremy Davey/SSC Programme Ltd., Jon Ferrey, Robert Laberge, LAT Photographic, Ken Levine, McKlein, Gavin Page, Mike Powell, Tamiya Model Company

▲ The best rally cars have four-wheel drive. This means that power is sent to all four wheels. This helps a car to keep going in bad conditions.

CONTENTS

⚙ **TECH TALK**
Look for the cog and blue box for explanations of technical terms.

👁 **EYE VIEW**
Look for the eye and yellow box for eyewitness accounts.

DAWN OF RACING

▲ Refueling a Fiat race car in 1912

There have been races since the early days of motoring, more than 100 years ago.

The first big motor race was held in 1895, from Paris to Bordeaux and back, in France. The winner drove at just 15 miles per hour (24 kph). This may seem slow, but at that time most roads between cities were little more than mud tracks.

⚙ BODYWORK SECRETS

Race cars are built around a strong body, called a monocoque. It protects the driver in a crash. It also supports parts such as the engine and wheels. You don't normally see the monocoque, since it is hidden behind outer panels. This race car has been stripped down. For racing, the colorful outer panels will be attached with screws and fasteners.

A metal roll hoop protects the driver if the car flips over in a crash.

The monocoque is made of light but strong aluminum.

Today that early race would be called a rally, an event that is still popular. Even so, most car races now take place on specially built tracks. The most important races are called Grand Prix, which are the French words for "big prize."

Different kinds of racing are divided into formulas. These are strict rules about how cars should be built. For instance, they state what their size and power should be. Officials called scrutineers check cars before every race.

◀ The driver lies almost flat in the car. Only his or her helmet sticks out of the cockpit.

GRAND PRIX RACER

Race cars are built with one thing in mind, to win races. So designers work hard to create cars that are light in weight and have powerful engines.

▲▼ In Formula 1 race cars, the engine is placed low behind the driver, hidden inside the body panels. It powers the back wheels.

The seat is shaped to fit each driver.

The body is made of carbon fiber, which is light but very strong.

Formula 1 cars are built around a light but strong body, called a monocoque. The word comes from the French for "single shell," because it is built in one unit.

Joined to the monocoque are the engine, wheels, and suspension. Airfoil "wings" at the front and back keep the car steady when it is driven at high speeds.

► Italy's Ferrari is the only Formula 1 carmaker that also makes its own engines. Most racing teams have their car and engine supplied by different companies.

Ferrari uses a black horse as its company logo.

The front wing pushes down to help keep the car on the track.

▼ Wide tires give lots of grip for turning corners at high speed. The small wing on top of the car has a tiny video camera inside. This way TV viewers can see a driver's view of the race.

PIT STOP

The pits are areas where race cars are serviced and refueled. In most races, cars need two or three pit stops. Cars in long-distance races may need more.

▲ A car's cockpit is a tight fit. Seat belts keep drivers in place.

▼ A top pit crew can refuel a BMW in less than eight seconds.

Pit stops have to be lightning-fast, and an unexpected delay may lose a driver the race. In just seconds, usually between six and nine, a trained pit crew can top up the fuel tank, change the tires, check the engine, and wipe the driver's helmet clean.

The car refuels from a tank in the pit.

▲ Air tanks blow up tires very quickly. Here a trailer is loaded, ready for a race.

⚙ CHOOSING TIRES

Racing tires come in two main types, one for dry tracks, the other for wet weather. Wet tires have a groove pattern cut into the rubber surface, so that water can drain away quickly. Dry tires are smooth, although Formula 1 tires now have four deep grooves. This is for safety, to slow the cars down in corners.

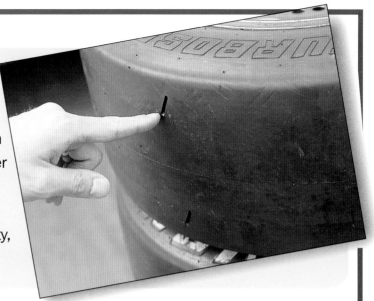

OVAL TRACK STARS

Stock car racing in the United States takes place on wide, oval tracks. Stock cars are modeled after sedans, except they have bigger engines.

▲ U.S. stock cars look a lot like sedans.

👁 THUNDER IN THE SUN

"Engine noise at a race often feels loud enough to blow your ears off! The pit crew uses ear protectors to avoid hearing damage. These protectors cut sound by more than half. The pit chief has a radio, so he can talk to the driver.**"** *Pit crew member*

The pit crew wears ear protectors.

U.S. stock car racing is a big test of drivers and cars. Races often last several hours. Regular pit stops and slow-downs to clear away crashed cars add to the thrills.

Wide tracks give drivers room to pass one another many times during a race. This is unlike Formula 1 races, where narrower tracks and more corners make passing less common.

◄ A Pontiac stock car reaches 186 mph (300 kph) on the straightaways.

◄ A huge crowd looks on as cars line up for the start at the Bristol Motor Speedway in Tennessee.

⚙ WHY DO SPEEDWAYS HAVE SLOPING CORNERS?

Stock car courses have banked (sloping) corners, so drivers can keep going fast. On a flat track, cars have to slow down much more for corners. If a driver takes a bend too fast, the car's tires will lose their grip, and the car may slide out of control. Banking reduces the danger of this happening.

24-HOUR RACERS

The most famous long-distance race is held at Le Mans, in France. Every year teams compete in a race that lasts for 24 hours.

◀ The Ford GT40 won Le Mans three years in a row in the 1960s. The rear opened so pit crew could service the engine easily.

▼ Le Mans race cars usually look similar. There is a central cockpit, with the engine behind. Powerful lights are needed at night.

Le Mans is one of motor sport's toughest challenges. The cars race flat out for the entire course, and leading cars may cover more than 3,100 miles (5,000 km) from start to finish. Many cars break down and never finish at all.

Bad weather is another danger, especially heavy rain. Dry-weather tires have little grip when wet, so it is easy to slide off the track.

👁 24 HOURS OF SPEED AND POWER

"Le Mans is somewhere every motor race fan should go, at least once. The track is made of ordinary roads, which are closed for the event. The noise and smell of the cars is something you never get anywhere else. Whatever the weather, the cars zip along at 250 mph (400 kph) or more. And there is an amusement park that you can visit in the evening!" *Le Mans visitor*

It is nearly sunset as a car roars under a footbridge at Le Mans. Racing carries on all through the night. On straight parts of the circuit, the fastest cars go about 250 mph (400 kph).

A single wiper keeps the windshield clear.

Caps seal the dual fuel tanks.

A radio aerial allows the driver to talk to the pit crew.

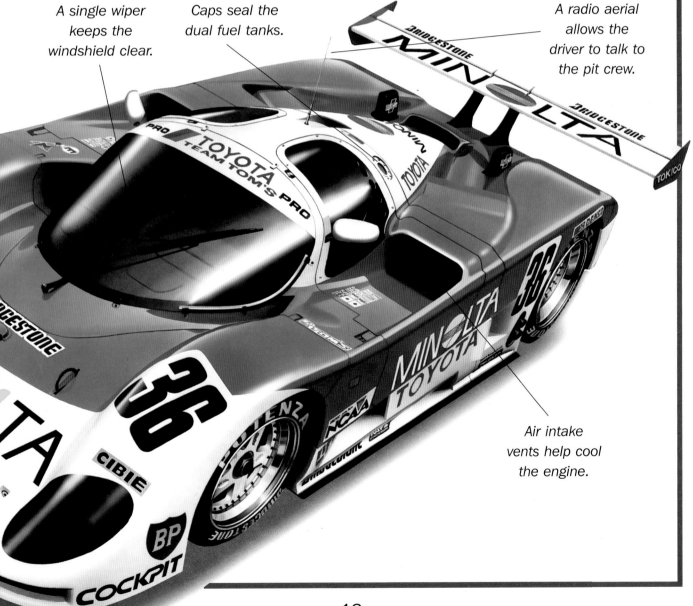

Air intake vents help cool the engine.

RALLY CHAMPIONS

Spare tires are carried on the roof.

▲ Drivers in the small but fast Austin Mini won the Monte Carlo rally three times in the 1960s.

Rally drivers race against the clock on courses that are made up of road and off-road sections. The biggest rallies cover thousands of miles.

The World Rally Championship is the most important rallying event. Drivers compete in rallies held in 14 countries across the world. Courses range from ice and snow in Finland to heat and dust in Africa.

The last race is in November, when the winner is declared. There is a break until January, and the Championship starts again.

⚙ KEEPING A GRIP

The fastest rally cars usually have four-wheel drive. This means that all four wheels are powered from the engine, so drivers can take turns quicker and get out of muddy spots more easily. If one or two wheels get stuck, the other ones can power the car out of trouble.

▶ People look on as a rally car speeds around a hairpin bend. Only top drivers get around tight corners like this without losing too much speed.

▼ A Spanish rally car throws up dust during the 1999 Safari Rally in Kenya. A metal grill at the front protects the engine from flying stones.

THE NAME GAME

Motor racing is big business. Many companies advertise by having their names painted on the cars. A company pays a racing team for this.

Big companies often back a racing team with money. In exchange the team advertises the company on their cars. This is called sponsorship. A top-class Formula 1 team needs more than $45 million a year to compete, so sponsorship is very important. And because racing is a worldwide sport, it is a good way of advertising to millions of people.

▲ The size of a sponsor's name depends on the amount of money donated.

👁 RACING BEFORE SPONSORS

"When my grandad used to watch racing, back in the 1950s, each country had its own color: Italy was red, France blue, the United States white with blue stripes, Great Britain dark green, and so on. It was a simple system, but they are more fun to look at today." *Race enthusiast*

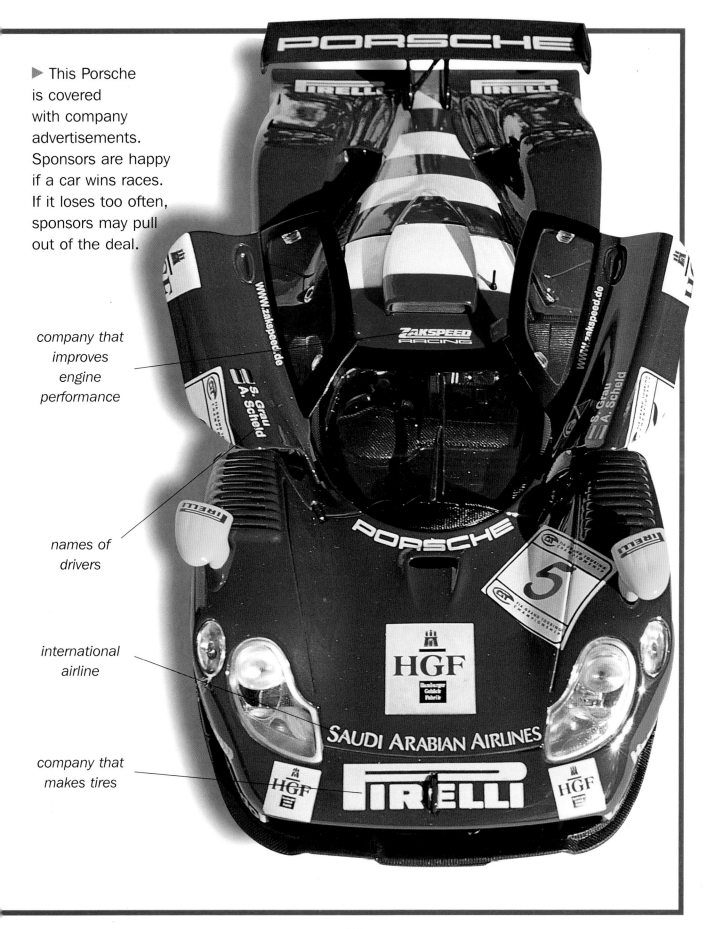

▶ This Porsche is covered with company advertisements. Sponsors are happy if a car wins races. If it loses too often, sponsors may pull out of the deal.

company that improves engine performance

names of drivers

international airline

company that makes tires

DRAGSTERS

A drag race takes place in a straight line. There is one quick blast down a quarter-mile (402-m) track. Then the race is over.

▶ Rear-engined fuel dragsters have huge back tires and tiny ones in front.

Drag racing is a speed test between pairs of cars. They line up side-by-side in front of a traffic-light "Christmas tree." Amber lights on the tree count down to green for "go."

With a mighty roar, the two dragsters race down the drag strip. The fastest can do the run in under four seconds. By the end, they are moving at more than 310 mph (500 kph) and have to use a parachute to slow down.

⚙ **BURNOUT BEFORE A RACE**

For the best acceleration, a dragster's tires need to grip the track well. Warm tires grip better than cold ones, because warm rubber is softer and slightly sticky. Drivers usually do a burnout before a race to heat the tires. Water is poured under the tires. Then they are spun fast. The result is a massive cloud of smoke as the water boils and rubber burns! Then it is time to race.

▲ It's burnout time before a race. As the tires spin, they warm up. They will give the best grip on the drag strip surface.

▼ A "funny car" has a body based loosely on the style of an ordinary car. This one has its engine in front of the driver.

air intake to engine

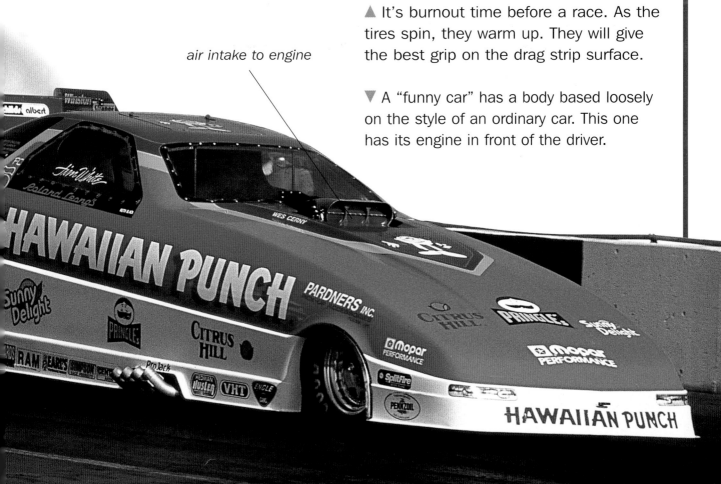

SOLAR CARS

▲ This solar car had a top speed of over 87 mph (140 kph).

Since the 1980s races between strange-looking cars, powered by the sun's rays, have become popular.

▲ The driver sits under a dark-tinted windshield in the GM Sunraycer. The two "ears" on top hold indicator lights and a system for seeing out of the back of the car.

Solar cars are almost pollution-free, because they do not burn fuel. Their power comes from solar cells, which change the energy in sunlight to electricity. This powers the electric motor.

Solar cells produce most electricity in bright sunshine. Then cars may speed smoothly along at 68 mph (110 kph) or more. On a cloudy day, drivers have to rely on their batteries. When these wear out, few cars go faster than walking speed.

Good weather for a solar race in Australia. Side winds from passing trucks can be a problem for lightweight solar cars. All entries have to pass a test first, to make sure they won't be blown off the road.

The first big solar race was held over a 1,860-mile (3,000-km) course across Australia, in 1987. Since then, the race has become a regular event, with teams from many countries taking part.

The cars come in many designs but share a basic smooth shape and lots of solar cells.

▲ This driver sits under a close-fitting plastic dome. The silver top reflects the sun's heat away from the driver's head.

▲ The 1999 Sunshark was built by students from an Australian university.

⚙ SUNLIGHT INTO ENERGY

Solar cells are usually made of a material called silicon. When light strikes silicon, an electric current is created. Wires from the solar cell can be connected to electric motors or batteries. Solar cells are used to power many machines, from calculators to satellites. Future cells may be strong enough to replace gas engines in cars.

LAND SPEED RECORD

▲ Bluebird was a LSR-holder in the 1960s.

One of the biggest challenges in motor racing is the Land Speed Record, or LSR. Drivers are timed as they zoom along on two runs.

Thrust SSC's driver sits in a small cockpit.

Thrust SSC has two powerful engines, one on either side.

In 1997 a car called Thrust SSC went supersonic, or passed the speed of sound, at 763 mph (1,227.985 kph). The driver was jet fighter pilot Andy Greene.

To set the record, Andy had 1 mile (1.6 km) to get up to speed, then was timed whizzing along another mile. Computer equipment confirmed that he was the fastest man on Earth.

▲ Thrust SSC's engines are warmed up before the start of a test run.

▲ Thrust SSC's driver, Andy Greene, has a cramped cockpit, packed with controls.

Thrust SSC has two jet engines. Before the car was built, they had been used in a jet fighter.

👁 BIG BANG IN THE DESERT

"We spent weeks in the U.S. desert. Thrust SSC went a little faster with each test run. On record day, we heard a double boom and knew Thrust SSC was supersonic. The boom is made by an object going so fast it crushes the air in front into an air wave that we hear as a bang." *Technician*

▲ Thrust SSC speeds across the desert, with the Black Rock Mountains behind.

▲ Thrust SSC is towed back to the start linc after each speed run.

23

FUTURE RACERS

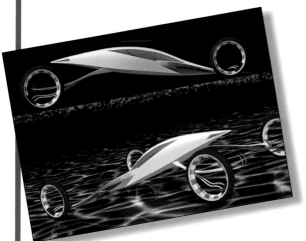

In the future, race cars may be built that are safer for drivers. Engines will make little pollution and will use less fuel than racers today.

◀ In the future, designers may use new materials to build strange-looking machines.

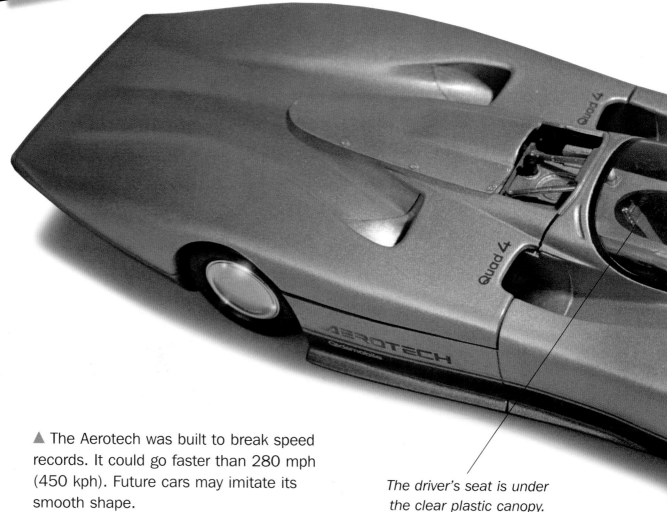

▲ The Aerotech was built to break speed records. It could go faster than 280 mph (450 kph). Future cars may imitate its smooth shape.

The driver's seat is under the clear plastic canopy.

Today's race cars use lots of fuel. A Formula 1 car covers only about two and a half miles for every gallon of fuel used. A small family car can go up to 20 times farther on the same amount of fuel.

New rules could force race car designers to develop engines that use less fuel. This should create cars that are better for the environment.

⚙ CLEAN METHANE

The gasoline (gas) we use as fuel comes from oil. When it is burned, it creates pollution. In the future, scientists may figure out a way to use methane gas as fuel. Methane burns cleanly, with little pollution. Japanese researchers think they may be able to use huge amounts of methane that is trapped in rocks below the seabeds.

Bodywork is built over a race car monocoque.

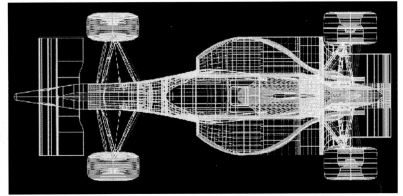

▲▼ Many race car designers use computers to design cars. They can try out all kinds of ideas before time and money is spent building the real thing.

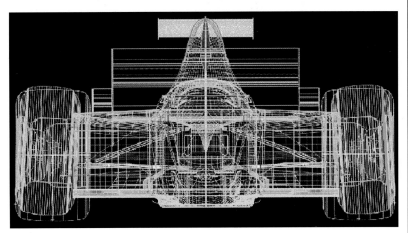

RACE CAR FACTS

Here are some facts and figures from the history of race cars.

◄ Drivers in this 1937 race had little protection, apart from gloves and a lightweight helmet.

First race

The first known car race in the United States was held in Wisconsin, from Green Bay to Madison. The route was 200 miles (323 km) long and was won by a steam-powered car.

Stopping to help

There were so many accidents in the 1903 Paris to Madrid race that it was stopped after the first day. The only female in the race, Madame du Gast, became a heroine for stopping to give first aid to injured drivers.

Deadly drive

In 1955 a car crashed at high speed during the Le Mans race. The driver was killed, and so were 82 spectators. It was the worst crash ever. Today race courses have crash barriers between the cars and the spectators.

Grand Prix winner

The driver with the most Grand Prix Championships is Juan Fangio, from Argentina. In the 1950s he won 24 races and was World Champion five times.

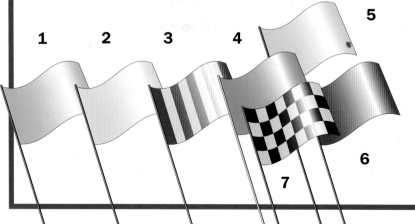

◄ Flags are used by officials to signal drivers during a race.
1 Car passing you.
2 Danger on track. Slow down.
3 Slippery track, probably oil.
4 Track now clear.
5 Slow service vehicle on track.
6 All cars stop at once.
7 Checkered flag, end of race.

A long way to go

Le Mans is a 24-hour race, so the faster your car, the farther you go in that time. The greatest distance ever traveled was 3,313 miles (5,332 km), by a Jaguar in 1988. It averaged more than 138 mph (222 kph).

Fastest dragster

The speed record for dragsters is held by American driver Gary Scelzi. In November 1998 he drove his car from a standing start to 325 mph (522.3 kph), in just 1,318 feet (402 m).

Safety first

Safety equipment carried in a car includes seat belts, a fire extinguisher, and a strong roll-over cage, made of thick steel. The roll cage takes the shock of landing, and keeps anyone inside the car from being crushed.

No steering wheel?

Grand Prix race cars have such small cockpits that the steering wheel is removable. It has to be, otherwise there is not enough room for drivers to get in or out!

▲ Motor racing is an exciting sport, but crashes are common. Luckily, the driver of this car escaped with only a few bruises.

A hot way to diet

Grand Prix driving is hot work, since the engine is just a short distance from the driver. On a warm day, the temperature in the cockpit can reach up to 122°F (50°C). During a race lasting perhaps 90 minutes, it's possible for a driver to lose weight simply by sweating.

RACE CAR WORDS

Here are some technical terms used in this book.

front airfoil

airfoil

A winglike part on a race car that helps keep the car steady even at top speed. Unlike an aircraft wing, which lifts upward, an airfoil wing pushes down, forcing a car onto the track.

aluminum

(a-LOO-mi-num) A silver-colored metal that is strong yet light in weight.

banking

Angled trackside at corners, used on speedway circuits in the United States. Banked tracks let cars go faster in corners.

burnout

A method of heating tires for a drag race. Spinning the wheels heats up the tires, which allows them a better grip.

carbon fiber

(CAR-bun FI-bur) The material used in bodywork and other parts of a car. Carbon fiber is usually a plastic with bits of carbon added.

circuit

(SUR-kit) Any closed track used for racing.

cockpit

The area where a driver sits. Seat belts keep a driver in place.

◀ A race car takes a corner at top speed on the banking of a U.S. track.

▶ A metal roll bar (*arrowed*) protects a driver's head if the car turns over.

crash barrier
(KRASH BEAR-ree-er)
Fencing that keeps cars from crashing into crowds.

ear protectors
Plastic cups like headphones, filled with material that absorbs sound.

formula
Rules that control how each type of race car is made.

Grand Prix
(GRAND PREE)
French for "big race." The term usually refers to Formula 1.

monocoque
(MAH-nuh-coke)
The center body of a race car.

petroleum
(puh-TRO-lee-um)
Fuel made from oil; a thick black liquid pumped from deep under the ground.

pit
The area where crews work on cars.

pollution
Chemicals put into the air after fuel is burned in an engine.

roll hoop
A metal hoop that sticks up behind a driver's head. If the car rolls in a crash, the hoop takes the shock of landing.

scrutineer
(skroo-ti-NEER)
An official who checks that a race car passes formula rules, so that it can take part in a race.

solar cell
Silicon material that changes the energy in sunlight to electricity.

sponsor
A company that pays a racing team for advertising.

stock car
A powerful U.S. car, modeled after a sedan.

supersonic
(soo-per-SAH-nik)
Faster than the speed of sound. This is about 758 mph (1,220 kph) at ground level.

RACING PROJECTS

These projects show you some of the science behind the world of race cars and motor sports.

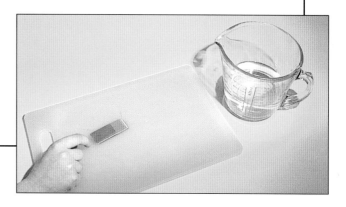

LOSING GRIP

Driving a race car is a battle to keep the tires gripping the track, especially on the turns. Losing grip may mean a car skids off the track and crashes. In wet weather, water makes the problem even worse.

1. You need an eraser, a flat board, and a pitcher of water. Flick the eraser across the board. It won't go very far before stopping.

rear airfoil   *front airfoil*

AIRFOIL ACTION

A race car airfoil works like an aircraft wing in reverse. It presses down, helping the car stick to the track. For this project you need a model car, thin cardboard, modeling clay, and a bathtub of water.

1. Cut out a small cardboard rectangle to make an airfoil shape. Tape it to the car's nose. Fill the bathtub with 4 inches (10 cm) of cold water.

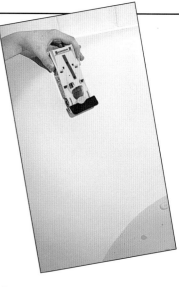

2. Angle the airfoil upward slightly. Release the car for a test run down the end of the bathtub.

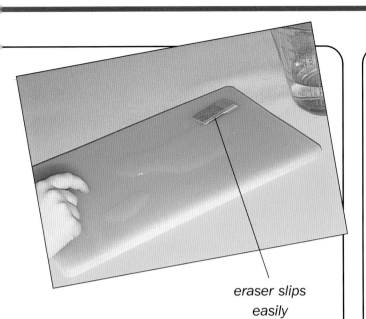

Near the engine is the noisiest place to be!

2. Now repeat, but wet the board first. You should see a big difference—the eraser loses its grip and slides easily.

eraser slips easily

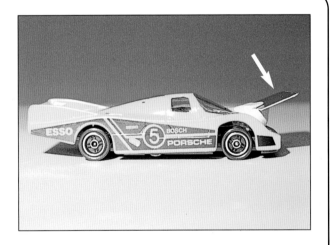

3. Water is thicker than air, so the test shows results at lower speeds than on a race track. At the airfoil angle shown above, the car lifts up. Try different angles to see which lift the car or hold it down.

SOUND LEVELS

Working in the pit is noisy. Pit crews wear ear protectors to protect their hearing. But just how loud is it? This list measures sound in decibels (dB).

33	Rustling of leaves in a breeze
45	Whispering one foot away
72	Talking between adults
77	In a busy fast-food restaurant
100	Roar of traffic in a city street
105	Jetliner taking off overhead
120	Near a race car in a pit

INDEX